Let's Go to a Stock Exchange

Bulls and bears aren't just animals to a stockbroker. Jackie and Graham learn some important facts about investments when they visit a stockbroker's office and later see how a stock exchange works.

Let's Go to a
STOCK EXCHANGE

by GORDON V. AXON

illustrated by FRANK ALOISE

G.P. Putnam's Sons • New York

"The bulls are really buying today," said one man.

"I bought mine at fifty," said another.

"It's up another point," said a woman.

Jackie and Graham were passing by a stock exchange in New York City. They were down on Wall Street on their way to the office of Mr. Hayes, their uncle's stockbroker. Mr. Hayes had promised to show Jackie and Graham around the exchange.

"Good morning!" said Mr. Hayes. "I suppose you've brought your investment money with you," he added, laughing.

Jackie looked surprised. Then she laughed, too. "I'm afraid we have only enough to buy our lunch, Mr. Hayes. But we do want to learn about the stock market since Graham and I have to write the financial page for our school paper."

"That's a big job," said Mr. Hayes. "Come into our office here, and we'll talk a little before we go to the Stock Exchange."

"What does a point mean?" asked Graham immediately.

"And I heard one man talking about bulls!" said Jackie.

Mr. Hayes laughed again. "A point, Graham, is simply another name for a dollar," he said. "And a bull market, Jackie, is the name we give to the stock market when the prices of stocks are going up instead of down. If a stock goes up one point, it is worth one dollar more."

"One man said he bought his at fifty," said Jackie. "Did he mean fifty dollars?"

"That's right," said Mr. Hayes. "And if his stock remains strong and the bulls continue buying, he will be able to sell it for a higher price than he paid for it."

Then Mr. Hayes explained that the men and women sitting behind the desks were stockbrokers. "We brokers," he said, "advise the people who come into our office about stocks and bonds. These people are investors," he went on. "They have invested their money by buying stocks and bonds. They want to know how much they could get if they sold their securities. Or how much they would have to pay if they bought some."

"We aren't even sure what a stock or a security is," said Jackie.

"Well, let's begin with securities," said Mr. Hayes. "That's what stocks and bonds are called. This is a big country full of thousands of companies. Companies issue stocks and bonds to investors. Some of these businesses are small. They are owned by one person and are called one-man businesses. A shop selling ice cream is usually a one-man business.

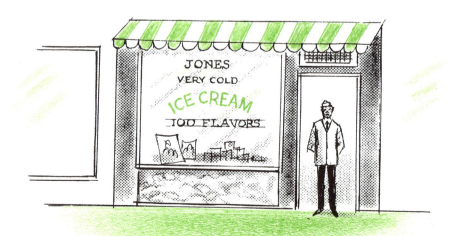

"But businesses get bigger and bigger. Sometimes, two persons, or three, or more will get together and form a business of their own. This is called a partnership. All the owners are called partners."

11

"My father has two partners in his television factory," said Graham.

"That's right," answered Mr. Hayes. "Now, let's suppose that this partnership does very well making television sets. So well, in fact, that the partners need more money to build a larger factory where they can make more television sets.

What do they do? They form a company. They tell their lawyer about it. He fills out certain forms and sends them to the capital city of the state. The state issues a certificate showing that a company has been formed. Let's call it the Sagamore Hill Company, Incorporated."

Mr. Hayes paused for a moment, looking from Graham to Jackie. "Do you understand so far?" he asked.

The children nodded.

"Fine," said Mr. Hayes. "The Sagamore Hill Company needs money. So it asks investors if they wish to put some of their savings into the company. Of course, these investors will want a certificate to show they've invested in Sagamore Hill. So the company issues two types of certificates. One is a bond. The other is called a stock certificate. Some companies issue only stocks and no bonds. But let's pretend that Sagamore Hill does both."

Jackie asked, "Why are there two types of certificates?"

"There's a good reason for two types of certificates, or securities," answered Mr. Hayes. "Some investors wish to make a loan to the company and hope to get interest on their loan.

They get a bond. Other investors wish to own part of the business. They get a stock certificate that shows how many shares of stock they have bought."

Jackie was puzzled. "I can see why there are stocks and bonds. But you said that people who

buy bonds get interest on their money. Don't the people who buy shares get anything?" she asked.

"They hope to," replied Mr. Hayes. "If the company does well, it will pay some of its profits to the stockholders. This money is known as a dividend. It all depends how well the company has done and how much money it has made."

"Suppose they lose money one year?" said Graham.

"In that case," said Mr. Hayes, "the company probably won't pay any dividends at all. But it would keep on paying interest on the bonds. That's why it's so important to understand the difference between a stock and a bond. A bond is a loan. Stock is a share of the ownership of a business."

"If a business gets bigger, does the price of the stock go up?" asked Jackie.

"Yes," said Mr. Hayes. "If a company does well and makes big profits, the shareholders, or stockholders, will get very big dividends. The price of their shares will go up. If the company loses money, the price of the shares will go down."

It was now Graham's turn to be puzzled. "You said that Sagamore Hill sold the stocks and the bonds. So why do investors need a stock-broker?"

"That's a good question," Mr. Hayes said. "You see, when the Sagamore Hill Company was first formed, it sold a certain amount of stocks and bonds. It may sell more later on, perhaps when it grows bigger. Meantime, any investor wishing to buy some Sagamore Hill stocks or bonds has to buy from another investor. He can't buy from Sagamore Hill since the company has sold all it wants to sell. That's where a stockbroker comes in. He buys and sells stocks and bonds for investors from other investors.

That's what our job is—buying and selling stocks and bonds for investors. Of course, a broker charges investors a fee every time he buys or sells. This money is called a commission."

"Is this a stock exchange?" Jackie asked, pointing to the brokers at the desks.

"No," said Mr. Hayes, shaking his head. "This office is a stockbroker's branch office. Our firm is a member of the stock exchange just down the street. In fact, we are members of all the stock exchanges in the United States, and we buy and sell stocks and bonds all over the world. Our firm is so big that we have other branch offices in many states. An investor in New York, or California, or Florida, or Illinois can go to one of our offices and give an order to buy or sell a stock or bond."

"Can anyone walk in, just like that, and give an order?" asked Graham.

"Yes," said Mr. Hayes, "just like that. But first of all you must open an account with us. It's just like opening an account in a bank. You simply sign some forms. After that, you are an investor and can give an order to buy or sell stocks and bonds. You can telephone your order. Or write a letter. Or send a cable. Or come in and talk to your broker."

Jackie nodded. "I think I understand now," she said. "Those brokers sitting at the desks here are taking orders from people who wish to buy or sell stocks and bonds."

"That's right," said Mr. Hayes. "We take orders from investors. Then we pass those orders to our brokers in the stock exchange. They meet with other brokers. That's where the buying and the selling take place—on the floor of the stock exchange."

"On the floor?" asked Graham, surprised.

Mr. Hayes laughed. "I'd almost forgotten how funny that sounds. The first time I heard it I remember thinking that a lot of men were sitting on the floor dealing out pieces of paper. I promise you that you'll see what it's really like when I take you over to a stock exchange later on. But first of all, you can see how we take an order here from an investor and send it to the stock exchange.

"Let's talk about Sagamore Hill again. Suppose an investor wished to buy 100 shares of Sagamore Hill, but did not wish to pay more than $15 for each share. He would tell his broker: 'Please buy me 100 shares of Sagamore Hill, but do not pay more than $15 for each share.' Or he might say: 'Please sell my 100 shares of Sagamore Hill, but do not sell them for less than $15 for each share.' His broker would make out a slip of paper: 'Buy 100 SGH at 15.' Or: 'Sell 100 SGH at 15.'"

"What does SGH stand for?" asked Graham.

"It stands for the Sagamore Hill Company, Incorporated," said Mr. Hayes. "But people are too busy to write out all those words. So each stock is given initials, just to make it easier."

Mr. Hayes took them inside the main office, and they sat around a desk.

"What's that noise?" asked Graham.

"That," answered Mr. Hayes, "is the ticker, or tape. It comes from a ticker-tape machine that makes a ticking noise and prints stock prices on a tape. There are hundreds of stocks. But just think of Sagamore Hill Company as SGH, and you'll get the idea. For instance, if you saw on that tape 'SGH 15,' it would mean that one investor had sold 100 shares of Sagamore Hill to another investor at $15 per share.

"Let's suppose you wished to buy 100 shares of Sagamore Hill. But you wanted to know the price of Sagamore Hill right now before giving

your order. That's where this other machine comes in. It looks like a television set. You simply tap out SGH on these keys here, and the present price of SGH is shown on this screen."

"Can you do that for a lot of companies?" asked Jackie.

"Yes," said Mr. Hayes. "For hundreds and hundreds. Now, let's say the price of SGH is 15. So you give an order: Buy 100 SGH at 15.

I make out a buying slip and put it in this tube. The tube takes the slip of paper upstairs to our teletype machine, which is like a typewriter. The operator of that machine types on the machine: BUY 100 SGH AT 15. This message goes to two places immediately. One copy goes to our head office. The other goes to our office in the stock exchange. Both offices have machines to receive these messages. Our broker in the stock exchange takes the order to buy and goes to see other brokers who might wish to sell Sagamore Hill. Usually, he finds one pretty quickly—at that price, $15. But they may not agree on price. If they can't, the shares are not bought, and the order is filed away to be used later."

"But suppose I really wanted to buy those shares," said Graham. "Could I buy them now at another price?"

"Yes," said Mr. Hayes. "But in that case you would say: 'Buy SGH at the market.' This means you are willing to buy 100 shares of Sagamore Hill and will pay whatever price is needed to get them."

Mr. Hayes stood up. "Let's have a look at a stock exchange now," he said.

"Yes, I'd love to see one," said Graham.

Before long, the three of them were in the visitors' gallery of a stock exchange, looking down.

"Remember the floor you asked about before?" said Mr. Hayes. "Well, that's it down there. It's called the trading floor. Those booths on the floor are called trading posts. Each stock is bought or sold at one of those posts. All the brokers know which stock is sold at which post. Sagamore Hill, for example, may be sold at that post there or at that one. All the brokers would know which one to go to."

"Those people down there," said Graham, pointing to the trading floor. "Are they all members of the stock exchange?"

Mr. Hayes shook his head. "Not all of them," he said. "Some of them are. Some work for the stock exchange itself. Others are hired by stockbrokers to help in the buying and selling of shares. You see, messages come here from all over the country, in fact all over the world, ordering brokers to buy or sell securities. So each brokerage firm has an office here."

"But who sends all the messages?" asked Graham.

"All the head offices and all the branch offices," replied Mr. Hayes. "It's a big part of the job of our staff here to collect the messages from their teletype machine and hand them over to our brokers on the floor down there. Sometimes, to save time, the order is given to the broker by means of hand signals from one of our staff on those benches that you see. In any

case, the broker gets the order and goes to the trading post where that particular stock is bought and sold, or traded—as we say."

Jackie looked at Mr. Hayes. "And at that post," she said, "that broker meets other brokers who also wish to buy and sell Sagamore Hill."

"You've got the right idea," replied Mr. Hayes. "That's what happens. As soon as the shares are bought and sold, the broker tells both the office staff and the exchange itself. The office staff sends a message back to the branch office by teletype. The branch office tells the investor who placed the order. Meanwhile, the exchange is telling all other investors what has happened. This is done by the ticker machine which prints out the tape you saw in our office. And that's all there is to it."

Graham asked, "Is it easy to become a member of a stock exchange?"

Mr. Hayes shook his head. "Any person wishing to become a member has to buy a seat of membership of the exchange," he said. "It costs money to become a member, and there are only a certain number of seats altogether. So a seat has to be bought from a member who wants to sell his seat."

"It looks like a pretty busy place," said Jackie, staring down at the trading floor.

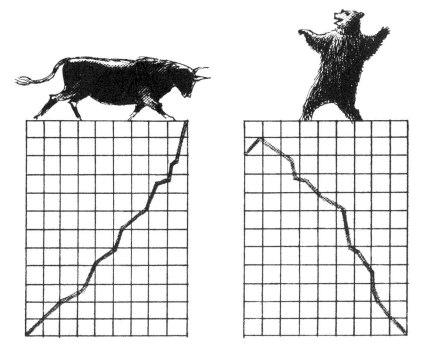

"It is right now," said Mr. Hayes. "Prices are rising, and investors are buying. They say the market is bullish today and may go even higher."

"We know about a bull market," said Graham. "But what do you call the market when the prices go down?"

"A bear market," answered Mr. Hayes.

Jackie and Graham laughed.

American Stock Exchange

TUESDAY, OCT. 3, 19??

Day's Sales	Monday	Year Ago	Year to Date 19??	19??
2,755,910	2,456,275	3,325,385	880,441,958	825,891,955

19?? High. Low.	Stocks and Div. Sls. In Dollars	Sls. 100s.	P/E	High.	Low.	Last	Net Chng.

A—B—C—D

19?? High.	Low.	Stocks and Div. In Dollars	Sls. 100s.	P/E	High.	Low.	Last	Net Chng.
36¾	20	AAR Corp	2	25	21¼	21¼	21¼	+ ¼
16⅞	11½	AberdMf .40b	5	7	12	11⅞	12	+ ⅜
4⅞	2⅛	Aberden Pet	5	17	2¼	2¼	2¼	
5¾	2⅞	Acme Hamil	13		3	2⅞	2⅞	
2⅞	1½	Acme Prec	3		2¼	2¼	2¼	
29½	17¾	Action Ind	28	22	21½	21¼	5¼	– ⅛
8¾	4½	Adams Russl	1	40	5¼	5⅛	9⅝	
10½	7½	ADM Indust	13	9	9⅝	9⅝	16⅛	+ ¼
24⅜	13	AdmirlInt .40	4	7	16⅛	16	5⅞	
8¾	4⅝	A&E Plast P	16		5⅞	5⅜	7⅛	
16⅞	7	Aero Flo .15r	2	9	7¾	7⅜	32⅝	+ ⅜
33	21¾	Aerolet .50a	60	16	33	32⅝	3⅞	
7¾	3⅞	Aeronca Inc	12		4⅛	4¼	3½	
5⅝	3⅛	Aerosol	1	162	3¼	3¼	13	
13⅞	5¼	Aerovox Cp	18	433	13½	13¼	8¾	+ ¼
12⅜	7	Affil Cap .52t	48	7	4½	4⅛	4½	– ¼
7	3⅞	Affil Cap wt			4⅜	4½	12¼	– ⅛
18½	11½	Affil Hosp .20	3	24	12½	12¼	12½	
14⅞	7	AIC Phot .56t	6	15	12⅜	12⅜	12½	
20⅜	12¾	Airborne Frt	29	21	9½	9¼	9½	– ⅛
13	7¼	Airpax 1.10t	9	15	9½	9¼	42½	+ ⅜
49⅝	17⅝	AlaxMag .60	13	41	42½	42¼	19¼	
27⅝	15	AlaP pf4.20	7	17	19¾	19¼	57	+ 1½
62½	55	AlanWd .40p			57	56	15¼	
25¾	15	Alaska Airl	z425		15½	15¼	6¼	+ ¼
9¾	4½	Alba Waldsn	9		6½	6¼	4½	– ¼
7⅞	5⅞	AlisnMt 2.85e	10		4¾	4¾	28¾	– ¼
28⅝	25¾	All Amer Ind	18		28½	28¼	3¼	+ ⅛
5⅞	3½	Alleghy Airl	51	10	29		14⅝	
25½	13	AllegAir pf C	2		3¼	3¼	44	– ½
74½	44	AllegA wtO	37	56	14¾	14	9⅝	+ ⅛
18	8¼	AllegA wtN			44	44	8	+ ⅛
14	7⅞	Allian T 1.05f	10		9⅝	9½	13⅛	– ⅜
23¼	13¼	Allied Art	9	7	13½		
7⅞	2½	Allied Th 1.10	62				
34½	26¾	Alpha Ind	1	10	26		
7	3½	Altamil Cp	38	8½			
9⅞	5⅛	Altec Corp	9	54			
2¾	1¼	Altec Cp wt	28				
2⅞	⅞	Alter Fds .50	20				
18¾	9¾	Alcoa pf 3.75	2	7			
54½	50	Amco Ind	z150				
18⅝	6½	A HessLL wt	2				
21⅜	10⅝	Am Agronom	37				
13	4½	Am Blltrt .40	8				
14¾	9¼	AmBook Stra	38				
	1⅞	A ConMts wt	6				
		Btch 2.64e	61				

Most Active Stocks

Tuesday, October 3, 19??

Company	Volume	Last	Net Chng.
Am Mot Inn	86,400	18½	– 1¾
Nat Paragn	85,000	21¼	– 2⅞
Telepromp	76,900	35⅜	– ⅝
Buttes Gas	44,600	20⅜	– ½
Guilford Mil	43,500	9¾	+ ⅝
TWA wt	39,600	24	– 1¼
WashPost B	32,400	31⅝	– 3/
Executone	30,400	23⅜	– 3½
Syntex	30,400	78⅞	– 3
Bankers Ut	29,300	19⅝	– 2?

19?? High. Low.	Stocks and Div. In Dollars	Sls. 100s.	P/E	High.	Low.	Last	C
52½	25⅝	Gulfstrm LD	21	18	28¾	28¼	28⅝
18½	8⅞	Hallcrft Hom	18	6	8¾	8½	8¾
11½	9⅛	Halls Mot .32	10	7	9½	9⅜	9⅛
9¼	6⅞	Hamilton Cos	2	13	7⅞	7⅜	5¾
8⅛	4½	HampsD .29t	6	9	5⅞	5¾	8½
14¼	7⅞	Hampt Sh .32	7	38	30	29¾	29¾
38¾	26½	Harland .13	19	30	29	28½	28⅞
35⅝	24¼	Harrahs .22	1	8	10⅞	10⅞	10⅞
13¼	8⅜	HartAlfrd .40	35	15	9⅞	9¾	9¾
17¾	9⅝	Hartfld Zody	11	43	23⅝	35¼	35¼
38½	30½	Hartz Mt Fds	7		2⅜	2¾	23
4¼	1⅞	Harvard Ind	15		5¾	5½	5⅝
7	3¾	Harvey Grp	2	12	3¼	3¼	3¼
7¾	3	Harvey St .12	4	25	16⅞	16¾	16⅜
24¼	12¼	Hasbro Ind	2	8	9¼	8⅞	9?
11¼	7	Hastings .20a	6	13	8½	5	5
10¼	4¾	Haydn Sa .20	4	8	5	5	5
13¾	6½	Health Chem	11	17	20⅞	20½	20
8¼	4¾	HealthM .30	9	28	4	4	
37¾	20⅝	Hecks Inc .08	56	10	13¾	13¾	13
7¾	2¾	Heinicke Inst	2	8	15⅜	15¼	
15⅝	12⅞	Heltmn 1.05e	2	12	11½	11½	
29½	13¾	Her Mal .48e	8		11¼	10⅞	
12¾	10⅞	HerffJon .05e			57⅝	56½	
		HIG Inc	92	18	6⅝	6½	
		Hill .30e		20	6¾	6⅛	

"No one seems to know just where the names came from, but many explanations have been given," Mr. Hayes went on. "For instance, a bear knocks people down, but a bull tosses them high. Frankly, I'm not sure myself why we say bull and bear."

Mr. Hayes looked at his watch. "Got to go," he said. "I have an appointment. You can stay here a little longer if you'd like. And call me if you have any questions."

"Thanks so much for your help," said Jackie.

"We certainly learned a lot," added Graham.

Jackie looked at Graham. Here they were, in the stock exchange, looking down on the trading floor. Some other visitors were listening to a guide telling them about the exchange.

"It's very exciting, isn't it?" said Graham as they left the stock exchange building.

"Yes!" said Jackie. "I still don't understand everything about stocks and shares, but I know more than I did an hour ago."

"A bull tosses prices higher," said Graham.

"And a bear pushes them down," said Jackie.

GLOSSARY

ACCOUNT — A statement given to an investor by his broker, showing amount of money lost and gained in the stock market.

BEAR MARKET — The name given to the stock market when stock prices are falling.

BOND — A loan from an investor to a company. The company pays the investor interest.

BULL MARKET — The name given to the stock market when stock prices are rising.

CERTIFICATE — An official statement to prove a fact.

COMMISSION — The fee paid by an investor to a stockbroker for buying or selling securities.

DIVIDEND — The payment made by a company to its stockholders.

INTEREST — The payment made by a company to its bondholders.

INVESTOR — A person who buys stocks or bonds.

SEAT — A membership in a stock exchange.

SECURITIES — The name given to stocks and bonds.

SHARE — The stock of a company is divided into parts called shares.

STOCK — Part ownership of a company. Also called common stock.

STOCKBROKER — An agent who buys and sells securities for investors.

STOCK EXCHANGE — A building where stocks and bonds are bought and sold.

TELETYPE — A machine that looks like a typewriter and is used to send messages from one office to another.

TICKER — The machine that prints the tape giving prices of securities.

TRADING FLOOR — The space in a stock exchange where securities are bought or sold—that is, traded.

TRADING POST — The booth on the trading floor where a particular security is sold.

WALL STREET — The main financial district of New York City.

Other Things To Do While Reading
Let's Go to a Stock Exchange

1. Look for articles on what is happening in the stock exchanges. Cut out such articles and paste them in a scrapbook. Write a short summary of each article underneath.
2. Draw cartoons about the stock exchanges, stockbrokers, and investors. Look for cartoons in the *Wall Street Journal* and other newspapers and magazines.
3. What are the two major types of securities? What is the major difference between them?
4. Draw a picture of the machine, found on a stockbroker's desk, that gives the latest price of a stock.
5. Write to a well-known company and ask for any free literature available to students.
6. Make a list of ten items, such as automobile and television set. Then put by the side of each article the name of a company in which investors can buy a share of the business on a stock exchange.
7. Visit a stockbroker's office and ask for a copy of any pamphlet available to students.
8. Look at the list of stock prices given in the financial sections of newspapers. Write down what each column means.

Other Books About the Stock Exchange

1. Brindze, Ruth, *Investing Money: The Facts About Stocks and Bonds.* New York, Harcourt, 1968.
2. Paradis, Adrian A., *The Bulls and the Bears: How the Stock Exchange Works.* New York, Hawthorne, 1961.
3. Sterling, Dorothy, *Wall Street: The Story of the Stock Exchange.* New York, Doubleday, 1955.

OTHER TITLES IN THE POPULAR *LET'S GO* SERIES

Science
to an Atomic Energy Town
for a Nature Walk
to a Planetarium
to a Rocket Base
on a Space Trip
to a Weather Station
to the Moon
to a Fish Hatchery

Health
to a Dentist
to a Hospital

Communications
to a Telephone Company
to a Television Station

Food and Clothing
to a Bakery
to a Candy Factory
to a Clothing Factory
to a Dairy
to a Farm

Commerce and Industry
to an Automobile Factory
to a Steel Mill
to a Paper Mill

Transportation
to an Airport
to a Freight Yard
to a Harbor
to a Truck Terminal
to Build a Suspension Bridge

Conservation
to a Dam
to a National Park
to Stop Air Pollution
to Stop Water Pollution

American History
to Colonial Williamsburg
to Mount Vernon
to an Indian Cliff Dwelling

Armed Services
to Annapolis
to the U.S. Air Force Academy
to West Point
to the U.S. Coast Guard Academy
Aboard an Atomic Submarine

Government — Local
to a City Hall
to a Court
to Vote

Government — National and International
to the Capitol
to the F.B.I.
to the Supreme Court
to the United Nations Headquarters
to the U.S. Mint
to the White House
to See Congress at Work
to the Peace Corps

Recreation
to an Aquarium
to a Circus
to a World's Fair
to a Zoo

Community — Commercial
to a Bank
to a Garage
to a Newspaper
to a Supermarket
to Watch a Building Go Up

Community — Government
to a Firehouse
to a Library
to a Police Station
to a Post Office
to a Sanitation Department
to a School

Geography
to Europe
to South America
to India
to Africa